KNOWLEDGE ATHLETE

Rui Zhi Dong © 2023

© Copyright 2023 by Rui Zhi Dong - All Rights Reserved

TABLE OF CONTENTS

Introduction	7
Developing Your Edge	10
Your Flavor	11
Your Love	14
10,000 Iterations	21
Focus	23
Expensive Mental Real Estate	24
Preparing The Mind	29
Be In The Moment	35
Action Drives Thoughts	38
Beliefs Drive Action	41
Put It Together	44
Adapt	47
Optimize	53
Optimize Your Environment	54
Optimize Your Cycles	58
Learning Principles	72
Learning Style	73
Get Clarity	77
Pareto Rule	82
Question	89
Relate	96
Learning Hacks	99
Modeling	100
Systems	106
Feedback	111

Conclusion	114
Additional Resources	117
Note-Taking Software	118
About The Author	119

INTRODUCTION

The game of life is the game of everlasting learning. At least, it is if you want to win. — Charlie Munger

Money is what fueled the industrial society. But in the informational society, the fuel, the power, is knowledge. One has now come to see a new class structure divided by those who have information and those who must function out of ignorance. This new class has its power not from money, not from land, but from knowledge. — John Kenneth Galbraith

When I first heard the term "Knowledge Athlete" from Naval Ravikant, it clicked immediately. It resonated with me because it means taking knowledge work to a new level of seriousness and professionalism in a world of cut-throat competition.

We live in a knowledge economy where we compete with essentially every knowledge worker around the world that has an internet connection (and I imagine with artificial intelligence at some stage). Simply getting a degree is no longer enough as the cost of information falls close to zero.

It's becoming more important than ever to focus on your unique capabilities and to improve your edge. My hope with this book is to help you develop your own unique edge, and to share with you the principles to outcompete as a knowledge worker. I've taken inspiration from professional athletes and tried to apply the principles from their world into the realm of knowledge.

When we look at the trends, it's clear that significant changes are afoot. Trucks are already driving themselves, tractors can harvest food with less and less human involvement, software with the help of AI can do the basic work of white-collar professionals such as accountants and lawyers. This trend will only grow stronger with time.

Fifty years ago, a passionate high school teacher that's better at explaining calculus would have had their talent limited to the size of their local maths classroom.

Today, that same teacher can reach billions of people through YouTube, and even make a good living doing so. Such a thing would have been unthinkable just one decade ago. As more and more viewers on YouTube prefer watching the person that's better able to explain concepts and ideas, this teacher ends up dominating the calculus niche.

The average calculus teacher, on the other hand, would probably only get a fraction of the viewership on YouTube, with all else being equal. Fifty years ago, this mediocre teacher would have done just as well as the talented teacher — both would be teaching at their local high school. This winner takes all effect will get even more amplified in the future as technology increases our reach and those at the top of their profession utilize advanced tools to become even more productive.

Technology enables massive leverage through infinite distribution and seemingly small differences in skills, judgment, and execution can lead to a disproportionately large impact and results.

Our best edge to thrive in a world shaped rapidly by advancing technology will be to focus on what we're uniquely suited for and do uniquely well.

Let's begin with developing your edge.

DEVELOPING YOUR EDGE

Your edge is something that builds slowly day by day, but surely, over time and compounding.

Within F1 Racing, the difference between first place and second can often come down to just a *fraction of a second*.

YOUR FLAVOR

Be yourself; everyone else is already taken — Oscar Wilde

Key Question To Consider:

- Am I being true to myself?

The best defense against competing with the masses is to focus on your individual strengths.

No one can compete with you on *being you*. To be more uniquely who you are and to emphasize the distinct flavors of your personality.

The following quote from Michael Phelps in his book, *No Limits*, comes to mind:

I never set out to be the second Mark Spitz.

I only want to be the first Michael Phelps.

I wanted to do something no one had ever done before.

That really resonated with me. I thought to myself, how much have I been true to my authentic self? How much has my journey been sidetracked purely by money or in response to how others perceive me?

I've had to give myself permission, over and over and over again, to be me. And to be okay with doing things my way, even when it mostly looks crazy or plain ridiculous to others. When I first started an online business in the early days of the internet and quit my comfortable corporate job, my colleagues thought I had lost it and that it was *never* going to work. Afterall, the expected life path back then was to get a university degree and then a good job somewhere. When you do something that's very different from what's expected of you, there will be pushback. It's human nature — we feel more comfortable in a herd where we are all moving in the *same* direction since that's generally increased our odds of survival. When you break away, it's lonely and uncomfortable.

That's certainly how I felt and why I needed to give myself permission to pursue what felt right, despite what others thought (and sometimes will made openly clear to me). If you're feeling the same, I now give you permission to be the most you that you possibly can be.

In a world where things are constantly changing, you need to have courage and belief in yourself to reinvent who you are when needed. Think about the professions that would have sounded absurd only 10 years ago like being a YouTube/Twitter/Instagram/TikTok influencer. Imagine, as the power of technology gallops along, how many more professions will get created within the next 10 years that would sound completely absurd today.

If you're working a job that you're always complaining about and you're really just there for the paycheck, you're probably not going to do the job as well as someone that absolutely loves doing the exact same activity and will end up with a very deep understanding of their specialty. Put another way, if you're doing well at a job that you hate, imagine how you'll do in one that you love. In the meantime, you're incurring an invisible cost of slowly putting out that flame you have inside of you that should be nurtured.

Look actively for ways to let yourself explore and grow without restrictions or limitations imposed on you by others or their expectations.

Unleash your potential by being true to who you are and letting your uniqueness flourish.

Follow your own nature and ignore the crowd.

YOUR LOVE

Key Questions To Consider:

- Where do I naturally gravitate towards?
- What am I naturally curious about?
- How do I spend most of my free time?
- How would I spend my time in an ideal world?

I have no special talent. I am only passionately curious. — Albert Einstein

The love of doing what you're doing can provide you with all of the fuel that you need to outwork and outcompete everyone else.

As a Knowledge Athlete, if you don't love what you're doing and you're only doing it for the money, and your competition is intellectually stimulated by their work, and they're addicted to what they're doing, then you're going to get outworked and outcompeted.

There's a great documentary, *Turn Every Page*, which focuses on the long-running professional relationship between the author Robert Caro and his editor, Robert Gottlieb — Caro is in his late 80s and Gottlieb in his early 90s. The title of the documentary captures Caro's approach to research and writing — he leaves no stone left unturned and examines every available source of information. There's one scene of Caro in the reading room at Lyndon Baines Johnson Library. He describes how he feels intimidated by the 45 million or so papers that's available at the library but his has a fondness for them because "once you start going through these papers, they're absolutely fascinating. I don't think there's anything I'd rather do than sit at one of those desks and just go through and find out stuff that's not filtered through a press release or some other books or something. I just wish I had several lifetimes so I could go through all of them."

To most people, this would look very tedious. He spends the whole day there for months on end just reading through all of the primary documents, files, and records available related to his book, hence "turning every page." He goes on, "Sometimes you're going through these letters and you say I'm going to look at a manageable number of boxes on some particular point — 8 or 9 boxes. It's going to take you a month or a couple of months. But you're going through one innocuous piece of paper after another just thinking, *am I wasting these weeks?* Then all of a sudden, there it is — the information that you were looking for. And it's there in writing. You see what actually happened."

The thing that keeps him going is that he's always fascinated. He says in the documentary that he "can't wait to in there [to the library]. Sometimes they tell you at 4:45 pm that you have to close your boxes and bring them up. And you can't bear to leave them and you can't wait to get in there the next morning. I've been doing this for 42 years. I *still* love getting in here in the morning." His books are a product of love. They've also won two Pulitzer Prizes in biography, two National Book Awares, among many others. His final book instalment in the series, *The Years of Lyndon Johnson,* is widely anticipated.

Caro's strategy is similar to that of the renowned investor, Warren Buffett. At the beginning of his career in the 1950s, he meticulously read through every single annual report of *all the publicly listed companies*, methodically going through them one by one in alphabetical order from A-Z. Again, this would look very tedious to most of us. This illustrates one thing Naval said which is that it feels like play to us, but looks like work to others. Susan Buffett, Warren's former wife, once said that Warren only needed a 50-watt light bulb and an annual report to be happy. You could leave him in a room all day and he'd be happy as can be.

The things that drive you towards a particular direction can be sometimes be more emotional than it is intellectual.

Pay close attention to what your actions tell you. They can give you clues about how you're really feeling about your work.

These don't necessarily stay the same over time. I enjoyed building my first eCommerce business immensely. Learning everything about product development, hiring the right people, getting the messaging right, figuring out logistics, and so on. I knew it was where I wanted to spend all of my time.

The second time around, I wanted to start a software company and eventually found myself unenthusiastic about having to recruit and manage people. I was instead drawn to reading and writing most of the day when I should have been focused on trying to grow the company. That's when I realized that it was no longer for me and made a change.

Be open-minded about wherever your journey leads you.

You have no responsibility to live up to what other people think you ought to accomplish. I have no responsibility to be like they expect me to be. It's their mistake, not my failing. — Richard Feynman

Just because you've spent many years on something doesn't mean you need to continue spending more of your precious time on. It's easy to get unwittingly drawn into a career that you've become an expert in simply by spending a lot of time with it.

If it doesn't feel right to you, dig deeper and reflect on it. Don't apply any pressure on having to achieve particular outcomes; instead explore with curiosity and listen to your intuition. See where the path leads you. While we all have responsibilities that must be taken into account, we also shouldn't go to the other extreme where fulfillment is fully given up for the sake of certainty.

In Paul Millerd's book, *The Pathless Path*, he talks about the difference between the "Pathless Path" and the default path. The former embraces uncertainty and permission to try non-traditional career paths rather than following any particular pre-defined paths.

When I left my "stable" high-paying corporate job to start an online business in 2010, my colleagues thought I was nuts. I didn't know anyone back then that did something similar and neither did my colleagues. Working in corporate was the acceptable career path, something you could feel proud to tell your friends and family during a barbeque. On the other hand, doing things online was not considered prestigious at the time — some people probably even viewed it as downright shady.

Many people choose professions based on what we think gives status and pays well. That's partially how I chose my initial career also. When I think about non-traditional career paths, Arnold Schwarzenegger comes immediately to mind. He grew up in a small village in Austria where he decided that he wanted to be a bodybuilding champion. His friends and family all thought it was a very bizarre and worrying pursuit — they were firmly against it. But he stuck with it despite what they all thought. After he won a whole lot of titles including seven Mr. Olympias, he decided that it was time for a new challenge. He had his sights set on being a Hollywood star. Again, no one thought this was going to work — here was this overly muscular beast with a thick Austrian accent, and he thinks he's going to make it, not just as an actor, but as a movie star? What a joke!

Of course, we all know what happened next — he goes on to become a successful action movie star. Eventually, he reinvents himself *again*, pivoting very much publicly to become the Governer of California.

I think it takes a deep-level of self-awareness to be able to reinvent yourself like that and to commit.

10,000 ITERATIONS

Key Questions To Consider:

- *Where* am I building my edge?
- Do I care about *how* I'm doing my work?
- Am I willing to *iterate* many times?
- Does the *process* spark joy?

In order to build expertise in anything, you need to get your repetitions in, just like in building muscle mass. You need to stay consistent and be in the game long enough for the iterations to compound your edge. In other words, you need to have *staying power*. Paul Graham once wrote, *If you find yourself competing with someone who could be described as an opportunist, you don't have to worry much. Opportunists, almost by definition, lack staying power. Usually all you have to do is keep going, and they'll fall away.*

Think about the difference between writing your first blog post and your 10,000th blog post. The difference between reading your first annual report and your 10,000th. Your first YouTube video and 10,000th.

In the early stages, more priority should go towards putting in your repetitions. You can spend all your time researching how to make perfect YouTube videos that go viral without ever making any videos. Or you can start making imperfect videos immediately and get real-time feedback.

Developing your edge will be easier if it's something that you love so that you're naturally curious about it and you're constantly working on improving your craft, regardless of the results or outcome.

In his book *Zen and the Art of Motorcycle Maintenance*, Robert Pirsig talks about taking his motorbike to a repair shop where a bunch of young guys are playing loud music while butchering his bike. For the kids, fixing the author's bike was just a mundane process to be over and done with. To Robert, each part of the bike expresses a unique function which together acts in symphony to produce motion and should be handled with great care and precision. Needless to say, watching the kids butcher his bike was painful for him.

How you do your iterations matter. You can put in your 10,000 iterations but if you're just going through the motions and don't actually *care* about how you're doing it, your edge is going to differ from someone that's doing the same thing, but with a lot of care.

FOCUS

EXPENSIVE MENTAL REAL ESTATE

I did not succeed in life by intelligence. I succeeded because I have a long attention span. — Charlie Munger

Free yourself from all other distraction. Do everything as if it were the last thing you were doing in your life, and stop being aimless, stop letting your emotions override what your mind tells you, stop being hypocritical, self-centered, irritable. — Marcus Aurelius

Every lap, you need maximum concentration. You need to focus 100%, so everything influencing your life must be in the right place and there can be nothing disturbing your mind. — F1 Driver

I've found thinking about my mind as real estate to be a wonderfully useful analogy.

Think of each thought that sits in your mind as having to pay rent. That thought needs to be paying the equivalent prices of the fanciest penthouse in Manhattan to have the privilege to occupy space in your mind.

Your responsibility as the landlord of this luxury penthouse is to monitor your guests throughout the day and ensure bad guests are kicked out *immediately.* No questions asked.

Key Questions To Consider:

- *Does this thought deserve to be here?*
- *Is it worthy of my precious brain cells?*
- *Why is this thought here?*

These questions are worth asking regularly **throughout the day**.

I spent a few days where I would try to note what my thoughts were every hour or so, without any judgement, on a physical notebook I'd keep with me at all times. I wanted to do a kind of "check up" of the mind. Needless to say, I found myself *very surprised.* I'd often catch incessant and aimless chatter, complaints about small things, self-criticism, wanting to check my phone for the latest on social media or the news, and worrying about things that will never happen. Aurelius would probably not be impressed. It was at this stage that I decided to be much more vigilant about the thoughts that occupied my mind. To treat my mind as precious real estate. Afterall, Aurelius tells us it's the *quality of our thoughts that determines the happiness of our life.*

Moreover, if my brain is going to be firing neurons anyway, I want it to be doing so on high quality thoughts of *my choosing*, not on random complaints or thoughts about someone that was being rude to me. Less brain power used on mental clutter means more brain power will be available for deep thinking.

To help me monitor my thoughts, I'd ask myself through the day, *Does this thought deserve to be here? Is it worthy of my precious brain cells? Why is this thought here?*

It's not easy to remember to do at first but it's well worth trying to develop the habit. You'll see just how easy it is for your mind to start wondering off. Just as you wouldn't allow a criminal to walk freely in and out of your home throughout the day, so you won't allow any negative thought to stay in your head for prolonged periods of time without your explicit consent.

You give energy to the thoughts that occupy your mind. The longer the thought sits there, the more energy thought consumes. We have a **limited amount of brain power** for the day so it's in your interest to catch the thought as soon as possible before it takes up even more precious resources. I mean, is it really worth giving brain fuel to thoughts about whether you were slighted by an acquaintance at a party for instance?

Negative thoughts that sit in your mind for a long time can start stressing you out and deplete your energy rapidly.

Other thoughts to watch out for are things for which you have **no control**.

For example, let's say that I buy $100,000 of shares of XYZ Company on the stock exchange and then the next day, it plunges by 50% on some bad news. I can stress all I want over declining share prices, thinking that, *Ah but if only I had purchased one day later, I would have saved $50,000! If only I had done things differently...If only...* But me thinking all day about it will make no difference whatsoever to the share price or, for that matter, to *what has already happened.* The stock market is what it is. The only thing I can do is either hold, buy or sell. That is **within my control**. The movement of the share price on the other hand is not within my control. The shares don't care whether I bought or not. It's not thinking, *Oh hey, I see can see here that you've lost $50,000 — let me see how can I make that up to you. All I ask is that you keep thinking about me.* It's only me that has personalized the entire experience.

I then remember to ask myself, *Why is this thought here? Does the thought deserve to be here?*

I'm having this thought because I feel pain at the "loss" (which is unrealized since I haven't sold the shares) and perhaps it has hurt my ego because I've internalized the market loss as a reflection of my intelligence.

The next step is to ask, **What's actually within my control?**

I can investigate what the news item is, see whether it's material to the underlying business, and perhaps revisit my original analysis of the company to determine whether it's still sound and whether any action should be taken.

Whenever you have negative thoughts, use it as a trigger for asking yourself: *Why is this thought here? Does the thought deserve to be here?*

PREPARING THE MIND

To make sure that athletes perform consistently at their absolute best, especially during intense competition, they need to be completely focused.

It's just as much a *mental challenge* as it is a physical one.

Research shows that the brain is not really able to significantly differentiate between a real memory and a visualized memory.

Dr. Michael Gervais, a sports psychologist sees the goal of visualization as "to create such a lifelike experience that your body believes that it could be real."

Visualization is a very common practice for world-class athletes. Charles Leclerc, Ferrari's F1 driver, says:

I've grown a lot mentally over the last few years... There are many techniques that can be used; I personally like the one of picturing the perfect lap in my head, especially before qualifying. I do this often because it really helps. When I'm not in the car this imagery helps me hugely to be fully concentrated and readapt to the car quicker.

So how can you, a professional knowledge athlete, apply visualization?

Just as athletes use visualization to ensure 100% focus, you can use it to ensure that your mind doesn't get disturbed so you can concentrate on your knowledge work.

Visualize your perfect day unfold, like a movie, while you sit still.

This usually takes me about fifteen to twenty minutes.

Key Question To Consider:

- *How would I like my perfect day to unfold?* (Visualise)

I generally prefer doing this exercise daily in the morning after I wake up with an empty mind and no stimulus yet to bombard me like iPhone notifications.

You can also do this exercise in the evening instead as you contemplate your next day. I reflect on how my current day played out in the evening, what went well, what could have been done better, which I'll do first before moving on to thinking about what are things that need to be done the next day.

A useful exercise to add on top of this is to imagine all of the things that could potentially go wrong and how you would handle those.

Key Questions To Consider:

- What are all of the things that can distract me?
- What are all of the things that can go wrong?
- How can I counter those things when they happen?

For me, it's things like the need to check my emails or social media during deep work that will derail my progress.

Or browsing YouTube or Twitter and suddenly losing 5 hours during the day...

I also know that if I go home, my habit is to unwind by loading up Netflix and snacking. Knowing this, I stay out at cafes and co-working spaces until *I've done what I need to* for the day. I can think that I'll finish up what I'm working on at home but it doesn't happen. So I set a little rule for myself that any work that *needs to get done is done outside of home.*

By creating a list of things *not to do*, you can become better at avoiding those things happening in the first place. And being better prepared to handle those things if they happen anyway.

When you go through your day and you run into something you didn't think of, you can simply add it to your list, as well as how you'll counter those things.

Mental Toolbox

When I first started writing, I'd spend days or weeks working on an article only for the article to be read by just a handful of people. After all of that effort, I sometimes started to think, *Why do I even bother?*

The bigger the disconnect between action and result, the easier it can be for self-doubt to creep in over time.

After a period of feeling sorry for myself, I eventually remembered that I'm doing something that I love. Writing helps me to think better and to gain clarity on my thoughts. It helps me get into the flow. It helps me to grow. So I have these in mind in advance for when I hit a mental road bump.

I'll have prepared in advance a range of different things I can turn to in times of self-doubt or when I'm just lacking motivation.

It can sometimes be as simple as listening to the right song.

Other times, I might think about Vincent van Gogh, who had been a disappointment to pretty much everyone in his life. He walked the countryside with no money at all, all alone, his clothes worn out. He would often sell his paintings in exchange for food and board (which would later sell for tens and hundreds of millions of dollars). Yet despite all of this, he kept going. He had given his life to his art. Nothing else mattered. When I compare myself to that situation, I realize that I've really got nothing to complain about while also being incredibly grateful for all of the comforts I have in life. And thinking about that works for me.

For times when I just need to push through, I might think about David Goggins and his, *I don't stop when I'm tired, I stop when I'm done.*

If I run into some unexpected problem? As Jocko Willink, the retired Navy SEAL Commander says, *Good, I have the opportunity to figure out a solution.*

Laptop is out of power? *Good, I can use pen and paper without distraction.*

Brainstorm Your List

You can think about what's helped you before when you've hit a snag.

Here are a few ideas:

- Recall a particular story that moves you
- Watch an inspiring YouTube video
- Imagining yourself as someone that inspires you
- Reading uplifting quotes
- Reading a positive self-talk script
- Going to a particular cafe that you love
- Going for a run in the park or exercising/stretching
- Playing a particular playlist
- Stream of consciousness writing

You can also look for new things to add to mix and adopt the ones that work better for you.

Then when you think through your day, and all of the things that could possibly go wrong, you'll also have a mental playbook ready for how you might handle any obstacles.

BE IN THE MOMENT

We have the ability to go in such a space, if you're willing to suffer, and I mean suffer, your brain and body once connected together, can do anything. — David Goggins

The best endurance athletes tap into a mental state of being *in the zone.*

They're purely in the moment.

They lose self-consciousness as spectators, officials and their competitors blur into the background.

It's just the moment. The present. The now.

Their fear of failure, their need to be perfect, their worries, their anxieties, their self-doubt melts away.

Their body and mind are in harmony.

Key Question To Consider:

- How do I get in the zone?

This answer will differ somewhat from individual to individual but the common factors are typically work that feels meaningful and challenging. For me when I write, it's some combination of the right environment, thinking about topics that I find interesting, and listening to music (very loudly!).

Consider how the following writers describe their writing experience:

When the sentences and the story are flowing, writing is better than any drug. It doesn't just make you feel good about yourself. It makes you feel good about everything. — David Baldacci

When I'm writing, I'm in an altered state of mind. — Sebastian Junger

I used to get the total immersion feeling by writing at midnight. The day is not structured to write, and so I unplug the phones. I pull down the blinds. I put my headset on and play the same soundtrack of twenty songs over and over and I don't hear them. It shuts everything else out. So I don't hear myself as I'm writing and laughing and talking to myself. I'm not even aware I'm making noise. I'm having a physical reaction to a very engaging experience. It is not a detached process. — Michael Lewis

Once you're fully immersed, it becomes easier to learn difficult things and focus on cognitively demanding tasks.

To stay in this state, you need to be able to focus without any distraction.

ACTION DRIVES THOUGHTS

Disable Distractions

Our smartphone serves as essentially *extensions* of our body with endless notifications and which make constant demands on our brain's limited resources.

Everything from Facebook, Instagram, Twitter to Emails, Slack Messages, News Notifications, Stock & Crypto price movements, etc. These notifications play on your brain's desire to seek novelty and makes deep thought difficult.

When you're in focus mode, disable all notifications if you can. The interruptions are just not worth it.

Protect your mind by keeping disturbances and any irrelevant stimuli to zero. The ideal scenario is to keep your phone on airplane mode while you're in high gear.

The same goes for multi-tasking.

Imagine that you're at a dinner party with music in the background playing. There are two people that are vying for your attention and both are speaking to you simultaneously — one complaining about their colleague at work and the other about their start up challenges. They're oblivious to each other, focusing only on you and whether you're listening. Now imagine doing that for 1 hour.

You'll not have heard as much as you would like to have and you'll feel pretty drained after just an hour. Why? Because you're basically just switching from person to person as oppose to listening to both at the same time (unless you're one of the rare ones). And trying to juggle this constantly will leave your brain feeling fried.

A number of research suggests that nothing affects focus negatively more than multi-tasking.

Drive Positive Actions

While checking social media may create negative thought patterns, making your bed can create a positive thought pattern. It leaves you with a small feeling of accomplishment and pride.

William McRaven in *Make Your Bed: Little Things That Can Change Your Life... And Maybe the World* argues that by simply tidying up your bed in the morning, you've started your day with a small success which helps set the tone for the rest of the day.

In addition to visualization, my morning routine consists of gratitude journaling on a physical journal, a bit of stretching or exercise and drinking lots of water. The little things count. Like keeping yourself and your surroundings clean, and not checking notifications.

BELIEFS DRIVE ACTION

You must expect great things of yourself before you can do them — Michael Jordan

Your beliefs become your thoughts, Your thoughts become your words, Your words become your actions, Your actions become your habits, Your habits become your values, Your values become your destiny. — Mahatma Gandhi

Key Questions To Consider:

- What are my most empowering beliefs?
- What powerful beliefs do I want to adopt?
- What are beliefs that have held me back the most?
- Deep down, do I truly believe that anything is possible?
- Do I accept full responsibility for everything that happens in my life?

Beliefs comes before choices, and choices comes before action.

Beliefs are powerful mechanisms that drive action, regardless of whether those underlying beliefs are true or not.

Thoughts create outcome.

Consider the 4 minute mile. Before it was broken, nobody thought it was possible.

After it was broken, it got broken regularly.

All it took was for one person to show that it's possible and the rest was history. It's the same with business as with pretty much everything else in life. Before anyone had multi-million dollar sales launches online, nobody thought such a thing was possible.

You can choose to believe that money is scarce or that money is everywhere. You can choose to believe in your own capabilities or you can choose to doubt yourself. You can choose to believe that rapid advancements in technology will destroy your career or that it will propel your career. The point being that you get to *choose* which beliefs to adopt and which ones to remove.

You can adopt beliefs that will create *desirable* actions or adopt beliefs that create *undesirable* actions.

Michael Jordan once said, "Never say never, because limits, like fears, are often just an illusion."

Consider what beliefs you have that may be holding you back.

The great thing is that you can choose which beliefs to uninstall and choose instead to replace them with empowering beliefs.

PUT IT TOGETHER

All of humanity's problems stem from man's inability to sit quietly in a room alone — Blaise Pascal

Imagine an athlete that's minutes away from competing in the Olympics and they're distracted thinking about what their partner said or whether they forgot to take out the trash.

That doesn't happen because they don't let their mind get disturbed. They're in the moment. They're focused. They have their game face on.

They've learned to protect their mind with maximum care and discipline.

F1 drivers don't necessarily require huge amounts of physical strength to outperform. But they do need to hit the exact spot consistently to the *millimeter* while driving at 200 miles per hour. All of this while processing huge amounts of information in real time and reacting accordingly during a long race. No wonder F1 drivers have very high rates of sustained attention spans.

One F1 driver once said, *Every lap, you need maximum concentration. You need to focus 100%, so everything influencing your life must be in the right place and there can be nothing disturbing your mind.*

Just as F1 drivers don't allow disturbances to their mind on the track, so why should you allow regular disturbances in the game of life as a knowledge athlete?

How you show up in your day to day life makes all the difference.

The way you approach your daily activities compound into something great. It's worth sweating the seemingly small details. Life's not one quick sprint but a marathon. It's how you manage your mental space, day in and day out, that will allow you to concentrate, focus, maintain long attention span, and ultimately succeed in the game of life.

But how can we protect our mind from mental disturbances?

We can seek to reduce them through meditation, journaling, actively monitoring our thoughts and treating our mental real estate as precious.

We can picture our perfect day, plan ahead for any obstacles we might face and be prepared to handle them swiftly.

It certainly takes consistent practice. But it's worth it.

The more you work on this mental muscle, the stronger it will get.

ADAPT

In today's rapidly advancing world of artificial intelligence, it's going to be very hard to be a knowledge worker and not utilize AI in the future. Its impact will, over a long enough time span fundamentally transform the landscape of the knowledge economy.

That means that it's going to impact everything we do — how we work, how we learn, and how we communicate. In a 2023 McKinsey report on Generative AI:

Generative AI's impact on productivity could add trillions of dollars in value to the global economy. Our latest research estimates that generative AI could add the equivalent of $2.6 trillion to $4.4 trillion annually across the 63 use cases we analyzed—by comparison, the United Kingdom's entire GDP in 2021 was $3.1 trillion. This would increase the impact of all artificial intelligence by 15 to 40 percent. This estimate would roughly double if we include the impact of embedding generative AI into software that is currently used for other tasks beyond those use cases.

Current generative AI and other technologies have the potential to automate work activities that absorb 60 to 70 percent of employees' time today.

When you have a game changer in the works, we must learn to recognize the signs and then be willing to adapt accordingly; we must be flexible in our thinking about how things are done and embrace wholeheartedly the changes as they come.

Leverage is a force multiplier for your judgement. Capital and labor are permissioned leverage. Code and media are permissionless leverage. — Naval Ravikant

Key Questions To Consider:

- *How can I leverage technology to learn better and be more productive?*

Technology gives knowledge workers unprecedented *leverage.*

It allows us to gain leverage through infinite reach and impact — think educational courses on Udemy to code on Apple's App Store to books on Amazon's marketplace.

It enables collaborative problem solving where smart minds around the world are looking for a solution from different angles — think Stack Overflow and GitHub which are widely used in the programming community. Stack Overflow is like the Reddit for programmers — users ask programming related questions and the most useful answer gets voted up to the top. GitHub is a collaborative development platform.

Technology gives knowledge workers unprecedented *productivity*.

AI today can automate repetitive tasks like document classification, report generation, continuously monitor data streams and so on. You can use AI to help you find very specific information in a large database of research papers. You can have AI analyze complex datasets and generate insights. I've used ChatGPT to quickly create all kinds of software to boost my own productivity — software that I would usually have to pay a developer to create. The possibilities are endless.

One area that's exciting is the impact of AI on medical research.

Researchers can identify gaps in existing research by using AI to scan through the current medical literature and uncover areas where further exploration might be needed. Medical researchers can also use AI to generate new hypotheses by synthesizing and analyzing vast amounts of scientific knowledge.

Medical researchers can also use AI to analyze large-scale biomedical data, identify patterns, correlations, and biomarkers that might hold crucial information for understanding various diseases. AI can then be used in predicting disease progression, treatment outcomes, and patient responses, giving valuable insights for personalized medical care and improving patient outcomes.

In order to take full advantage of the increasing power of AI, Knowledge Athletes need to become fluent in the technology and stay updated on what's happening. This is a rapidly evolving field, and new technologies and techniques will continue to emerge.

This can include studying the architecture of large language models like GPT-4, experimenting with them, understanding how they can be applied to your knowledge work, and being aware of where their limitations are, such as hallucinations and data privacy concerns. The tools itself will no doubt change. The most important thing is knowing what the goal is and leveraging the right tools that will help get you there. Part of this means having an understanding of what each tool is good at and what they're bad at.

Renaissance Technologies, one of the most successful quantitative hedge fund in the world, uses AI to make money consistently year after year from market inefficiencies. They have large teams of scientists that have programmed their algorithms to process at least several *terabytes* of data per day to enable their AI to make profitable financial trades.

Zillow on the other hand built a property-flipping business on AI that was meant to predict property prices and buy the houses the AI thought was undervalued. This project ended up being a disaster, costing the company hundreds of millions of dollars and 2,000 lost jobs.

So what went wrong with Zillow? While they had a ton of data, the data collected was over a relatively short period of time. Market cycles can run over a *long* time and since they held onto properties longer, they were more subject to the larger macro force. Furthermore, there was probably specific knowledge about the individual properties that locals knew about but the AI didn't.

At a high level, one can argue that AI has a better advantage on very short-term trading in financial markets because there's a lot of data to process over the short-term. This can include all of the recent and historical micromovements of the individual stock price, the same data on competitor's stock prices and overall indices, the weather, any newly released government economic repors — and these are just to name a few! In Renaissance's case, that adds up to several terabytes of data a day. Imagine a human trying to process all of that!

The point is that in order to fully utilize AI, Knowledge Athletes needs to understand where the current limitations are and whether there are solutions to overcome them. It's going to do some tasks extremely well and others not so well.

Knowledge Athletes must remain flexible in their approach, adopting a generalist mindset when it comes to the tools that will help them reach their goal.

Knolwedge Athletes are curious, possess a lifelong habit of learning, remain open-minded, and are always ready adapt to rapid changes to stay ahead of the curve.

If you're just getting started, you'll find that there's a wealth of information available online including on YouTube and highly active AI communities that are very keen in helping others understand and learn.

OPTIMIZE

OPTIMIZE YOUR ENVIRONMENT

Key Question To Consider:

- How Do I Make My Environment Work For Me?

Keep your physical surrounding clean.

Unnecessary stuff can distracts us from focusing on the task at hand. It can be as simple as putting away your Playstation so that you're not tempted every time you're in the living room and having to exercise your willpower unnecessarily.

You can also take an intermediate step if you don't want to go cold turkey. For example, let's say that you're working from home and you want to stop your Netflix usage because you're spending too much time watching TV when you're suppose to be working. One option would be to remove or throw away the TV altogether. If that feels too much, then you can also make it a bit harder to watch Netflix by using an older streaming device that loads everything very slowly. Then one day you may just decide that you won't bother loading Netflix at all anymore and work instead.

Find out what kind of environments work for you, then aim for that. For me, I work best in a noisy cafe that's ideally buzzing with energy and people, has bookshelves filled with books and a cozy interior decor. When I stay at home, I get lazy and don't feel like doing anything. Knowing that, I aim to be out of the house as soon as possible in the morning. I have my first cup of coffee or tea outside always.

For you, it could be the exact opposite where you're most productive at home. It could be about turning your home office or private office space into an inspirational place to work from by rearranging some furniture, adding some plants and having a nice stand up desk. Or just trying out more spaces in your area.

Browser Clutter

If you're working on various browser tabs to get stuff done, close the ones that aren't strictly relevant for what you want to do and especially any distracting tabs that updates automatically like News sites, Gmail, Messenger and so on.

If you have a tendency to let your tabs go out of control like me, you can use a browser tab management system to try and organize your tabs into the different projects that you're working on. While seemingly small, keeping your tabs organized is a good way to staying productive and minimizing distractions.

Once you've finished for the day, close all of your tabs. You can bookmark them, add them to a document, to your to do list or just deal with it on the spot (like finish reading a 5 minute article). The issue when you start your day with a browser full of tabs is that they remind you of all the things that need to get done, like emails, and are a mental distraction. Better to start with a fresh new browser window.

You can take it to the next level by thinking in advance what tabs you'll be using the next day and keeping only those open so that when you turn on your computer, it's the first thing that you see.

When I turn on my MacBook, the first thing I see is Roam Research, the software I use to take notes and to write generally.

This helps me keep a daily writing habit so that I don't need to think, *Now what should I do?*

For example, I kept the material for this book open in Roam Research last night so that I would continue working on it today.

If I'm working from home, I like to keep books around the working area. In cafes, I'll always take a few books with me and place it on the table next to my laptop. Something about having the books there helps inspire me.

Experiment with what works best for you and optimize accordingly.

Remove anything that's likely to distract you.

OPTIMIZE YOUR CYCLES

Timing Your Activities

Lions lay around most of the day resting in the shade. They will store up energy for short intense bursts of hunting where they can run extremely fast for short periods to capture their prey. They tend to be more active and hunt around dusk and dawn.

Similarly for humans, our cognitive abilities will fluctuate throughout the day. Daniel Pink, author of *When: The Scientific Secrets of Perfect Timing*, "Our performance varies considerably over the course of the day, and what task to do at a certain time really depends on the nature of the task [...] If we look at the evidence, we can be doing the right work, at the right time."

For most of human history, our work has generally been seasonal and it's unnatural to work robotically during all of our waking hours. It's unrealistic to expect that we maintain peak performance consistently at all hours of our workday. If you're finding that you constantly need to take coffee (or other substances generally) to stay alert, you're masking the problem.

Chronotypes

Chronotypes are determined by the circadian rhythm and the best way I've found to figure out which type you are is just by monitoring your mood throughout the day.

Top performers are well aware of their chronotypes and will do everything they can to align their activities according to their energy cycles.

Each day will have a trough, peak, and recovery.

For me, as a night owl, I start the day in recovery mode where I have an uplift in mood but I'm generally less energetic. This is the period when my creativity is at its best because the better mood plus less interference from my analytical brain means tapping more into my imagination. I use this period to write as well as think about big ideas, brainstorm, reflect, consider solutions.

It's the time of day that I may ask myself questions like, *What Am I Missing? What Are The Low Hanging Fruits?*

If you're an early bird, then this phase is likely to come later in the early evening.

Then comes the trough which typically happens in the early to mid-afternoon. This is when your mood is low and it's the time to do things like checking messages, social media, replying to emails, and so on. I usually use this period to go for a jog, work out in the gym, a walk in the park, go for a swim, then followed by the sauna.

This resting period is usually the time that I'll get those "Aha!" moments after a burst of creative energy in the morning. Despite stopping creative work in the morning, the subconscious brain will continue working in the background and I've tried to intentionally order my routine so that I'm more likely to get these moments and big ideas consistently.

Ernest Hemmingway was known to stop writing in the middle of a sentence and call it a day.

Learned never to empty the well of my writing, but always to stop when there was still something there in the deep part of the well, and let it refill at night from the springs that fed it. I always worked until I had something done, and I always stopped when I knew what was going to happen next. That way I could be sure of going on the next day. — Ernest Hemmingway

This reminds of Thomas Edison's *Never go to sleep without a request to your subconscious*.

For me, the modified version is *Optimize your rest by making a request to your subconscious* while making sure there's still fuel in the tank.

I like to push during my creative hours but not *too much*. The feeling I'm going for is a kind of pleasant exhaustion.

Finally comes the peak when I'm in high gear and focused. This is the period when I'm highly productive. I use this period to do analytical work including anything research oriented as well as power through anything that needs to get done. For instance, I might come up with some ideas as well as an outline for a blog post in the morning and then actually write the post itself later in the afternoon.

At a very high level, here's how my day roughly looks:

10 am: Wake up, morning routine and then head to cafe. Read a bit of philosophy (generally the works of ancient philosophers), do some reflection and writing. Will do creative work like brainstorming.
2 pm: Workout (e.g. jog, bike, weights) followed by sauna/rest. Then lunch.

4 pm: Functional work like research, more writing. Other activities like marketing, administrative work, zoom calls, making videos and so on will get done during this period also.

8 pm: Dinner and winding down. Journaling and preparing for the next day.

I'll try to maximise the amount of walks I do in between these activities which I find helps with my thinking. For example, there's a cafe very close to where I live but I purposely walk a bit further to the next cafe to get the blood flowing.

Order Matters

I've played around a lot with changing the order of what I do and monitor how I'm feeling and my energy levels. I might try doing functional work followed by exercise and see what that feels like. It's amazing how something as simple as just changing up the order of things can have such an outsized impact.

Mixing things up and then monitoring is a great exercise to get to know your own body and its cycles. You can start with just *one thing* and focus on that for a week or two. For example, if you typically meditate in the morning, then try meditating in the afternoon instead and see what happens. If you typically eat breakfast, see how it feels when you skip the first meal. If you typically workout in the mornings, try switching it to the afternoon.

Stress and Rest

A core part of athletic training is the idea of Stress + Rest = Growth. We apply the appropriate amount of stress to the system, then we allow it to recover.

Similarly, we can apply intellectual stress by exerting mental effort in learning something new or in doing something intellectually stimulating or creative. This, combined with proper rest, allows neural pathways to get strengthened, especially after exposure to new information.

When applying intellectual stress, I like to think about high intensity interval training. The physical training is intense, explosive, and exhausting. But you also feel satisfied afterwards for having done it.

When doing knowledge work, the high intensity equivalent is something that's mentally challenging, requires immense concentration and focus. Regardless of whether I've got a knowledge project that I'm working on, I make sure that I do at least one very challenging mental activity each day. Of course, you can also overdo it.

If an athlete overtrains, they run the risk of injury or burnout.

Similarly, knowledge workers that go too far will suffer from mental fatigue and reduced productivity.

The key is in finding the balance that works for you. Listen to your body and mind. The most important thing is making sure that you have adequate rest.

Rest

Cycles go on throughout the day, through the week and throughout the year.

While many of us are great at applying stress during work, most of us don't pay enough attention to *resting* that's just as important, if not even more so.

Athletes can easily train everyday if they wanted to. But they *consciously* choose not to and instead force themselves to strategically rest and recover after intense training. Similarly, knowledge workers need to be similarly disciplined in applying rest into their routine.

We need rest during the day (afternoon slump), rest during the week (weekend), and rest during the year (holidays).

Daily

To make sure you remember to rest during the day, you can have it as a part of your routine or block it out on your calendar, depending on what works for you. You can use this time to, for example, take a nap, go for a walk in the park, go to the sauna, and so on. I personally enjoy going to the sauna as a daily ritual for rest and recovery. In addition to the health benefits, it also helps me to clear my thoughts and reset.

Sauna

I like to use the sauna as part of my *daily routine* followed by a cold shower or cold plunge, depending on what's available to me at the facility I'm using. I'm sure to a lot of people, this will sound like a lot. It's not something that I would actively recommend to everyone but I find that it works for me. If I'm working out at the gym, I'll use it as part of my post-workout recovery. If not, then I'll go after a walk in the park or a light jog.

Part of the health benefits of using the sauna is that your heart muscle contractions are improved, the stiffness of your arteries are reduced to accommodate the increased blood flow from using the sauna, there are certain cognitive benefits, and it improves your mood. In short, you get improvements to both your physical and mental well-being. What's not to like!

There was a study conducted (*Association Between Sauna Bathing and Fatal Cardiovascular and All-Cause Mortality Events*, April 2015) with 2,315 Finnish men over the course of above *21 years* to see what happens when saunas were used regularly.

The ones that used saunas 3 times per week were 24% less likely to die during the course of the study. If they used the sauna 4 to 7 times per week, they were 40% less likely to die.

Whether you spend this time in a sauna or in some form of nature like the park, take advantage of this time by being digitally disconnected and fully detached. This will help you to reduce stress and anxiety while giving your brain a chance to reset.

Cold Exposure

In addition to cold exposure after going to the sauna, I generally take cold showers daily for a minute or so while inhaling deeply through the nose into the belly and exhaling softly through the mouth.

Cold exposure can improve immunity levels, increase blood circulation, burn fat, reduce inflammation and improve your mood.

One way to get started with cold showers is by having small amounts of exposure — say 5 seconds at the end of a warm shower and then increasing it slowly over time.

Weekly and Monthly Reset

The Japanese have a term *shinrin-yoku* which means "forest bathing." The term emerged during the 1980s when the government wanted to connect citizens to the nation's forests and to prevent burnout. The government then conducted over a hundred studies to see what kind of benefits shinrin-yoku offers.

In one of the studies, they found out that people who spent 15 minutes sitting and walking through nature experienced decreases in heart rates, stress hormones and blood pressure. After two hours in the forest, people with high levels of stress experienced large drops in anxiety and depression. Some studies showed diabetics whose blood sugar rates returned to regular levels after sustained doses of nature.

This research spurred the Finnish government to investigate further by surveying thousands of their citizens. Around 95% of Finns spend their time outdoors and the government wanted to know how much time spent outdoors was... *optimal.*

The study found that spending 5 hours a month was when people felt best in a country where they experience long and dark winters.

I think that when you have down time during the weekend, it's nice to spend at least a few hours in nature. And then once a month, stay a few days in the wild outdoors. If you're tight on time, then ideally aim for at least once a month visit to nature. The wilder the nature, the better.

5 hours can be a picnic, a hike, a bike ride.

Annual Reset

When I'm thinking about longer rests, the person that immediately comes to mind is Jerry Colonna. He's the co-founder of an executive coaching firm, Reboot, and he's been taking *2 month* sabbaticals every year for the past decade.

The word sabbatical is related to the same root word of sabbath which means a day of rest.

For me, this is a time of thinking differently. Of getting in touch with myself. During the normal working year, I'm focused on achieving my goals and the shorter rests have been to recharge and rejuvenate.

For the larger annual breaks, I explore and wonder with childlike curiousity. I use the time to work on something other than what I've been working on. But there are no expectations. No goals to accomplish. No pressure to achieve something. The most important thing is just to take it easy.

Taking extended breaks will not always seem practical. That's okay. Find something that *does* work for you and your situation. You can start small and take it from there.

Consumption versus Production

Just as there's a time to push and a time to rest, so there's a time to consume and a time to produce. A time to be creative and time to be productive. A time to be focused, where you're actively trying to understand or figure something out, and a time to be diffuse, where you're more relaxed and thinking about concepts on a big picture level. A time to explore and a time to exploit.

Consider where on the spectrum you are right now. How much time do you spend on a day to day basis acquiring knowledge versus being productive?

My focus right now is 90% on producing and being productive by gathering my thoughts and writing this book.

When the pendulum swings back into knowledge acquisition mode, I'll go down the rabbithole for a few weeks or months on whatever I find intellectually interesting. It might be on something that happened in history, understanding some new technological innovation or reading about a particular topic in the sciences, typically in biology or physics.

The cycles can look very different depending on what you're doing. Consider when Bill Gates was still the very busy CEO of Microsoft. The majority of his year was *productive*.

He would then shift focus by taking a week off during his annual "think week" just to read books. He'd fly off to Hood Canal and spend a week there all alone, just thinking and reading. He would take a big bag of physical books and technical papers. No laptops, digital reading devices or interruptions.

Understand where in the cycle you are. Just as by working during what's meant to be your rest period, you up neither resting properly nor working well, so jumping back and forth between being creative and being productive will be just as ineffective.

Ask yourself, *Is this a situation for creativity or productivity?*

Is this a situation for exploring or for exploiting?

You also don't want to be spending too much time only on one end of the spectrum. The entrepreneur Alex Hormozi once said something along the lines of, *Beginners overvalue thinking and devalue doing. Advanced people do the opposite.*

Key Question To Consider:

- How can I make this feel easy? What would that look like?
- How can I make this *work for me*?
- How *often* will I do this? How will I make that happen?

LEARNING PRINCIPLES

LEARNING STYLE

Key Question To Consider:

- How Do I Learn Best?

Knowing how you learn best is an important thing to know about yourself.

You'll spend a significant portion of your life learning, so it's good to know how you learn best so that you can let your learning advantage compound over time.

There's no sense in forcing a style that doesn't suit you.

The fact is that most people just have no idea the best way they learn.

John F. Kennedy was a **reader** who assembled a group of brilliant writers as his assistant and made sure that they wrote to him before discussing their memos in White House meetings.

This is a process worked well *for JFK*.

Lyndon Johnson on the other hand was a listener. But he didn't know this and with the same people on staff as JFK, his staff followed the same process and they just kept on writing.

He apparently never understood what they wrote. It wasn't his style.

On the other hand, as a senator, Johnson performed well since being a good listener works to his advantage in the senate.

There are four primary learning styles.

Reading

Warren Buffett reads 20-25 books a week in addition to reading newspapers and journals on a daily basis.

He has near photographic memory and has no need to take notes.

He once said that he doesn't listen to podcasts generally because it's an ineffective use of his time. He's far more effective at reading than he is at listening, and he sticks with what he knows works best for him. In other words, Buffett is well aware of his own strength and he stays with where his strength is.

Listening

I have a friend whose first instinct when learning a new topic is to talk to people. He never remembers what he reads (it just never clicks the same way) but has an amazing ability to understand when he's listening.

Writing

Beethoven left behind a huge amount of sketchbooks which he never looked at.

He once said, "If I don't write it down immediately, I forget it right away. If I put it in a sketchbook, I never forget it and I never have to look it up again."

Speaking

Sometimes I like to talk to my partner for hours on end about a topic.

I would talk over different points of view each time and go into a lot of details. I would sometimes ask questions but generally I'm just thinking out loud.

That's how I'm learning, thinking and processing.

Key Questions To Consider:

- *What is my learning style?*
- *What's the best way that I learn?*

You need to figure out how you can best accommodate your learning style, and act accordingly.

You don't need to completely exclude one method or the other. You can emphasize the learning method that works better for you. The key is figuring out what **works best for you** and sticking with that. This way, you can let your learning advantage compound daily.

Study hard what interests you the most in the most undisciplined, irreverent and original manner possible. — Richard Feynman

Disregard the one size fits all approach and play to your strengths to develop your unique edge.

GET CLARITY

Key Questions To Consider:

- What's the goal or purpose?
- What outcome do I want?
- What does success look like?
- What are the main questions that I would like answered?

Before you start your learning journey, it's good to get clarity on what you want.

Learning with a clear goal as opposed to learning aimlessly will improve your focus.

It's perfectly okay to say that you're just curious about a topic and want to explore. You also don't necessarily need to solve it immediately either. Richard Feynman, a famous theoretical physicist, Nobel Prize winner and author of several books, liked to keep a mental list of his favorite problems at the back of his mind. Then whenever he reads about a new trick or technique, he would test it against one of his problems to see if it helps.

The key here is just to be aware of what you're after so that you're not mixing it up with something like trying to acquire a specific skill, making a presentation, or writing a non-fiction book for instance since they would take a different approach.

Having clarity means knowing whether you can extract the information you need from specific sections of a book or reading book summaries instead of having to read books cover to cover. Many of us think we *have* to read a book from start to finish simply because that's *always* how we've done things, even when it doesn't make sense to do so.

Knowing what you want will help you determine the approach to take and chart a course accordingly.

The more specific and more thought out your goal, the better.

Consider the following examples and the approach you'd take for each goal:

- I want to learn marketing (Not Clear)
- I want to learn the fundamentals of copywriting and apply tested principles in my digital advertising business to increase conversions (Clear)

- I want to learn AI (Not Clear)

- I want to get a high level understanding of the current state of research in AI (Clear)

You can also get more specific after some general research and narrow down to something like *I want to understand the most exciting trends in Computer Vision and NLP areas.*

Build The Roadmap

- What is progression of learning makes the most sense?
- In what order should I learn the blocks of knowledge?

Once you have a clear goal in mind, you can build your roadmap. This means spending some time in doing a bit of high level research.

Think of it as building a mental map of the undertaking. Of getting a lay of the land.

The essence of this is in trying to get the big picture and then filling in the details later.

A good example of doing this is Mortimer Adler's approach in studying a non-fiction book.

Here are a few ideas based on his book, *How To Read A Book*:

- Carefully study the title
- Study the table of content
- Study the blurb
- Read book summaries
- Deduce overall argument structure
- Get a handle on the big ideas in the field through general research and learn to build your own outline.

Getting a handle on the big ideas is a useful practice to do since you won't always have a table of content to work with when you're working with non-book formats like long lectures, and a lot of authors won't necessarily do a very good job on their table of content.

You'll also be able to relate all of the information that you research according to your outline thereby strengthening your ability to understand, relate and retain information that you're processing.

Additional ways to help you build a mental map:

- Reading book summaries
- University course outlines
- Existing mindmaps on the subject
- Searching online forums and checking Reddit
- General overview research on Google
- Watching general YouTube videos on the topic
- Talk to subject matter experts

This list is certainly not exhaustive but will hopefully give you some ideas on getting started.

PARETO RULE

Key Questions To Consider:

- What's essential?
- What are the big ideas?
- What are the fundamentals?
- What don't I need to know?

Another reason why knowing the goal and what you want is useful because you can then figure out what's essential and what's not.

You have clarity.

In an age where we have access to unlimited information, the key thing is to have a good filter and good judgement to determine what's core and actually important. According to a New York Times article, we consume up to 34 gigabytes of data *per day*. If we lose sight of what's important, it's easy to feel overwhelmed from information overload.

The Forcing Function

Having a constraint can be very useful. When we have a constraint, we come to the realization that we don't need to consume absolutely every... tiny... bit... of... information.

- How would I approach learning this topic if I had to do it in 4 months, 4 weeks, 4 days?

When I spoke to Knowledge Athlete Tiago Forte about constraints, the author of *Building A Second Brain*, he said the following:

I actually find it helpful that I have constraints. I finish every day around around 2 or 3 pm because that's when I need to pick up the kid when daycare is over. I just have to be much more intentional, much more picky about where I allow my time to go. The time I spend organizing and re-architecting my note-taking system which I love to do, or organize it in some new fancy way where I'm going to add more links and more tags and all.

You can kill a start up by giving it too much money because all discipline goes out the window. They don't have to prioritize, they don't have to hire well.

It is really bad to have unlimited of any resource including information and time. People always say, "If I had more time, I would write my novel or do my big goal." I doubt it. I doubt more time by itself would make any difference.

When you're reading a book, is it more important to read every single word and try to memorize everything, every single fact and figure, or to focus on the **big ideas**?

For example, there's a very popular book written by Ben Graham many years ago on value investing called the *Intelligent Investor*.

The most important ideas from that book is about the markets being irrational and having a margin of safety.

If you read that book without an understanding of the essentials, you might get lost in all of the details about different stock selection strategies and come out not remembering anything useful.

Of course, what the important key ideas will actually be for you will depend on what your goal is.

Pareto Principle

When you're doing your planning and learning, remember to apply the Pareto rule in filtering information.

The Pareto principle, named after the Italian economist Vilfredo Pareto, is also known as the 80/20 rule. It states that 80% of the consequences come from 20% of the causes. The essentials are the 20% that tell you most of what you need to know. We don't need to read every single sentence of a book to get the big ideas.

Figure out what the big ideas are.

Know the basics, the fundamentals, very well and master them.

Then you can build upon a strong foundation and grow your branches of knowledge from there.

The goal is **deep understanding**.

Not vanity metrics like the number of words read or how fast you can read. You can read many books without understanding much of anything.

You can know the name of that bird in all the languages of the world, but when you're finished, you'll know absolutely nothing whatever about the bird. You'll only know about humans in different places, and what they call the bird. — Richard Feynman

You do not really understand anything unless you can explain it to your grandmother. — Albert Einstein

A good test to see whether you truly understand a topic is to use the Feynman Method.

The Feynman Method

Richard Feynman could explain any fundamental physics concept from scratch with simply a pen and paper. In one of his lectures, he essentially explains mathematics from *counting* to precalculus by building up an unbroken chain of logic, all from the top of his head.

He had an incredibly deep and fundamental understanding of his subject. The goal of the Feynman method is to communicate concepts using concise thoughts and simple language.

If you can't explain an idea or concept in your own words and in simple terms, then you haven't fully understood them.

One useful practice to test your understanding and check for gaps is using the Feynman method as follows:

1. Choose a concept you want to learn about
2. Pretend you are teaching it to a student in the sixth grade.
3. Identify gaps in your explanation. Go back to the source material to understand it better.
4. Review and simplify
5. Use analogies to explain your understanding

Let's consider the sentence, *the soles of your shoes wear out because of friction.*

How would you rephrase that?

Here's how Feynman demonstrates it in very simple terms:

Shoe leather wears out because it rubs against the sidewalk and the little notches and bumps on the sidewalk grab pieces and pull them off.

Simple, right? But you can see that this shows true understanding.

It's also **vivid**. Our brain is far better at learning and remembering through **vivid imagery and stories that evoke emotion** rather than the purely abstract and theoretical.

When learning the new essential concepts, try using stories or grounding what you're learning in practical and concrete terms.

Key Questions To Consider:

- *What's essential?*
- *What are the big ideas?*
- *What are the fundamentals?*
- *What don't I need to know?*

Figure out what the big ideas are, look to truly understand the essentials, and test your understanding by rephrasing it simply.

If you need to memorize it, then you haven't really understood it. If you haven't understood it, then you're not going to use it and you'll soon forget ever having learned it.

If you need to use a lot of big words for your explanation, go back and restudy your material. As Albert Einstein once said, *if you can't explain it simply, you don't understand it well enough.*

QUESTION

Key Questions To Consider:

- What claims are being made?
- What evidence is used for such claims?
- How strong is the evidence?
- What's not there?
- How do I know this to be true?
- What information is surprising for me? Why?

You should always carry a healthy dose of skepticism during the learning process. Einstein once said that *education is not the learning of facts, but the training of the mind to think*. He was a proponent of critical thinking and questioning the established ways of learning and teaching.

When interacting with any kind of information, it should never be a one way street where you're just digesting information passively as if you're watching Netflix.

It ain't what you don't know that gets you into trouble. It's what you know for sure that just ain't so. — Mark Twain

I have steadily endeavoured to keep my mind free so as to give up any hypothesis, however much beloved (and I cannot resist forming one on every

subject), as soon as facts are shown to be opposed to it. — Charles Darwin

This applies not only to things you're learning but to what you already know — your assumptions, your beliefs. The things you hold to be true. While the notion that the Earth is not flat seems obvious today, it was very difficult for most people to accept this (and still is for some people) for a long time. When people only saw white swans, people reached the conclusion that *all swans must be white*. That is, of course, until some Dutch explorers spotted black swans in Australia. We need to treat all knowledge *as subject to change until new evidence arrives*. That's partially why the philosopher Sir Karl Popper thought science should not be taken too seriously and that knowledge does not always increase with additional information.

While this of course is easy to understand in theory, it's difficult in practice. There's a saying that *science progresses one funeral at a time* from the German physicist Max Planck. The reason is that it wasn't the great physicists of the time that heard new ideas (ideas which oftentimes conflicted with their own) and then became convinced by sound arguments that advanced science. Rather it was their *death* that cleared the way for a new generation of physicists more open to radical new ideas and had less attachment to the existing ways of thinking that helped move science forward. Until they too eventually became the old guard, attached to the existing ideas and a new generation would once again come along to challenge them. And remember that we're talking about *very smart* world-class physicists. If they're prone to irrationally holding onto ideas that no longer make sense, it's safe to say that the rest of us probably have similar tendencies.

Be aware of your psychological biases including confirmation bias. *We all have them.* It's really just a matter of working daily towards having slightly less bias and trying to be a bit more rational.

We regularly form ideas and beliefs in our head and then we go on to look to confirm what we already believe, and often unconsciously disregard anything that contradicts it. This is made worse if our entire career is dependent on a certain way of thinking (as was the case with the physicists).

Charlie Munger once said that, *Any year that passes in which you don't destroy one of your best loved ideas is a wasted year.*

The mindset that helps me is to think of myself as a detective and imagine that I'm constantly in some kind of dialogue with my material, with the primary goal of **deepening my understanding of reality**. To figure out what's actually true.

A good example is how the hedge fund Bridgewater Associates, a $140 billion asset manager, operates. Known for their culture of "radical transparency," they seek to answer just two questions:

1. *How does the global economy work?*
2. *How do you take that understanding and utilize it to build great portfolios?*

Having only two questions as their *primary focus* over their decades of operation gives them a lot of clarity and helps them figure out what's important and what's not. Everything they learn, they write down. It helps them accumulate concentrated knowledge and apply them to the markets. They put their learnings down in the early days on yellow pieces of paper and, with the progress of technology, eventually translated their understanding into algorithms.

Greg Jensen, the co-chief investment officer of Bridgewater says, "We've refined our understanding of quantitative easing, just by **staring at what's surprising us**, building that into the process, and you keep moving [...] All of the time, there are things happening in the world that are surprising us and then the new research is all focused on those surprises, and things that we haven't already built in. [T]hat's what we study, and we keep studying and keep evolving" (the emphasis is mine).

Key Question To Consider:

- *What's surprising?*

A significant part of their approach is to actively look for things that are *surprising*. A way of essentially focusing on contradicting evidence. This helps to avoid the natural human tendency of seeking to confirm what they already believe but rather, actively search for data points that would question their understanding of reality and how markets operate. To essentially stress-test what they think they already know and update their thinking, or their "compound understanding machine," when necessary.

When I'm listening to a podcast, reading a book or having a conversation, I'm constantly on the lookout for *what's surprising*. I'll give you an example just from today. There was an interview I listened to where the founder of a remote jobs board website (remoteok.com) was saying a significant portion of his revenues are corporate clients spending on average $50,000 *per transaction*. The reason why it's so high is because they're buying bundles of job posts. But the reason I found it so surprising is because there's no sales person involved in closing the deal. It all happens online without any interaction with a sales person. The customer just puts $50k on their corporate credit card the same way I might buy paperback books on Amazon. This runs counter to my **assumption** that high ticket online transactions requires a sales call of some sort for the sales to occur. The next question for me are:

-Is my assumption wrong?
-Is this a unique case or can this be extrapolated into other types of online businesses?
-If so, what kind of online businesses and how?

Of course, this is a different topic altogether and outside the scope of this book.

Authority Bias

Another thing to keep in mind is that just because you read something in a well-known book or heard it from a smart person doesn't necessarily make it true. The bias to watch out for is authority bias where we tend to blindly believe experts, even when what's claimed is pure nonsense. Even more so when so called experts are quoted, sometimes out of context, in the media.

Your approach is that of a skeptic.

You don't accept anything at face value.

Everything comes under scrutiny. You're an independent thinker.

For example, when you're taking online classes, what you're doing is validating claims.

The course instructor says that x is y. Now how do I know that to be true? How does the instructor back up the claim?

Keep an open mind and question everything.

RELATE

Key Questions To Consider:

- How does this fit in with what I know?
- Does it complement, confirm or contradict?
- What is it similar to?
- What are the differences?

You can't really know anything if you just remember isolated facts and try and bang 'em back. If the facts don't hang together on a latticework of theory, you don't have them in a usable form. — Charlie Munger

Always look for ways to relate what you're learning to what you already know. Think about how the different ideas and concepts relate and hang together. This process helps us build a mental framework of the knowledge we're acquiring for better retrieval and usage.

Look for linkages. Things that are similar, things that are different.

Imagine a tree trunk and you're adding branches.

Each new piece of information is a branch you're adding or modifying.

If it's not directly linked to anything you know, consider any patterns. Anything it reminds you of. Or how it's different to something. Or maybe it's analogous to something.

For example, in engineering, there's a factor of safety that's used for constructing bridges to make sure that it has an additional buffer for any unexpected loads.

Usually the minimum for this is 2x. This is similar to the Ben Graham's investing concept of margin of safety.

The more you can make links to what you already know, the more you can understand and retain.

Your framework for making sense of the world will become bigger and over time will enable your knowledge to compound.

One cool hack for relating information is to get a blank sheet of paper and create a mindmap of everything you know about the topic. Let's say that the topic is investing. The main concepts we've briefly touched on are margin of safety and the psychology of markets.

Then when you read a book on the topic or watch a lecture, use a different colored pen and relate the new information to what's on your mindmap. In this case, let's say that we're reading a section about hedging strategies which talks about how we can protect our portfolio during a market panic. This information can be related to the psychology of markets since financial markets would be exhibiting a lot of fear during a meltdown.

Now if we actually know investing well and want to specifically learn about advanced hedging strategies as our *primary focus*, then instead of a general mindmap on investing (which would be too broad for our purpose), we can create one on hedging strategies instead and write the big ideas we know on the topic. The mindmap you go with is dependent on the amount of knowledge you already have on a given topic and what your focus is.

LEARNING HACKS

MODELING

Key Questions To Consider:

- Who are my ideal Knowledge Athletes? Why?
- How can I best model these Knowledge Athletes?
- How do these Knowledge Athletes produce results?

Modeling is a simple yet incredibly powerful way to replicate what others are doing. It means seeing anyone in this world that has produced a result that you want, you can seek to produce the same result by modeling them.

Jazz legend Clark Terry advocated a 3-step approach to learning the art of jazz: imitation, assimilation, and innovation.

Imitation is about listening, absorbing the feel, the expression and the tempo of your model artist. This would typically be artists that you love and adore. Assimilation is about synthesizing and internalizing the rhythms, the nuances, the harmony. Innovation is about making it your own.

Just as Clark Terry told his students to model their favorite jazz artists, so you can model your favorite Knowledge Athletes.

Consider your model Knowledge Athlete as your unofficial mentor. *How do they get the results that you want? What habits do they have? What beliefs do they have? What is something surprising that they do?*

One of the Knowledge Athletes that I try to model is Charlie Munger (probably not surprising given how often I've quoted him!). He reads voraciously, understands a diverse range of subjects from physics to psychology to architecture to economics intimately, and is an independent thinker (he also happens to be a billionaire, which doesn't hurt!).

It's easier to study Charlie than his better known business partner at Berkshire Hathaway, Warren Buffett, because he tends speaks his mind without much regard for what others think of him. With Buffett, you often need to read between the lines to understand what he's *really* thinking since he's much more diplomatic and will often avoid saying things to not cause controversy or create shocking headlines.

To model Charlie, I'll first thing about what it is about him that I admire and what results I want to replicate. I'll then listen to his talks, read any books about him, attend Berkshire Hathaway conferences, and take detailed notes along the way.

Here's a simplified version of how I might answer some of the questions about my unofficial mentor:

How do they get the results that you want?
- By studying the big ideas from the big disciplines
- Avoid doing stupid things and being overconfident
- Minimize psychological biases and try to be rational.

What habits do they have?
- Spends most of the day reading, learning, and thinking.

What beliefs do they have?
- That we need to recognize reality even when we don't like it.

What is something surprising that they do?
- He reads university textbooks for fun.

I want to thoroughly understand Charlie's thinking such that I can answer the question, *What would Charlie do in X situation?*

The better you can answer this question, the better you yourself will be able to model your Knowledge Athlete and get the results you're looking for.

Another Knowledge Athlete that I admire and try to model is Ed Thorp. He started off as a maths professor in the US and was living month to month without any savings. One day he got curious about blackjack. Using his maths background, he figured out a way to game the system to his advantage. He eventually wrote a paper and published a book about his findings. Suddenly he found himself with some spare cash from book royalties and his winnings from blackjack. He decided to teach himself investing, found a way to exploit anomalies in the stock market using his knowledge in probability and statistics, and made a fortune. On each occasion, he was following his intellectual curiosity, which is something that I myself try to model.

The way he puts it is, *I was an academic and I was curious and I found things interesting and I wasn't really in there to get rich. I was in there to deal with interesting math problems that kept coming up like blackjack. Roulette was a maths/physics problem. Investing for me was lots and lots of math. So I enjoyed that. I just do things I like. I don't worry about money. Do what you love and the money may follow and if doesn't, you're still doing what you love.*

Key Question To Consider:

- Who do you want to model?
- Why do you want to model them?
- What do you most admire about them?
- How do they approach learning?
- How do they produce the results that you want?

The best place to start is with anything that they've personally written (like an autobiography or books generally, blog etc.) as well as any interviews they've done on podcasts or YouTube. I try to think about it as if I'm mentally having coffee with the person I'm trying to model.

As I'm reading through their autobiography, I'm asking questions like, *Why do you think this? How is this similar or different from my own thinking? What would I do in this situation?* If there's a particular medium that you enjoy more, try to emphasize that during your learning. Generally, I prefer the immersion approach where I'll read, listen, and watch my model Knowledge Athlete to really feel like I know them.

Oftentimes, the expert may be open to an interview where you get the opportunity to pick their brain, whether in academia or in industry. It can also help if you have a podcast or YouTube channel.

I've found many Knowledge Athletes on Twitter and LinkedIn that I've reached out to by messaging them directly. Sometimes they may not have direct messaging enabled in which case you can build relationships by replying to them thoughtfully on Twitter. You can also try emailing them.

I've found that many are very generous and patient so don't be afraid to reach out!

SYSTEMS

Key Question To Consider:

- What systems can I adopt to help achieve my goals?

Scott Adams in his book, *How to Fail at Almost Everything and Still Win Big*, talks about why systems are more effective than goals for getting what you want. He writes that, *Goal oriented people exist in a constant state of failure or waiting for the goal. Systems people win every day just by sticking to their systems. The systems focused people tend to perform better and be happier.*

Adams never set out with a specific goal to become a best-selling author. He just started writing while responding to feedback from readers. He did more of what they liked and less of what they did not like. Similarly with weight loss, it's smarter to have a system of becoming better educated about nutrition, eating better and tracking food instead of just having a goal of losing X weight.

Similarly for knowledge, there are many systems that can be adopted to enable better learning, information storage, creativity and insights.

If you're not already in the habit of regular learning, that'd be the first system to set up.

How can I set up a system for learning that best suits me?

Instead of saying that my goal is to read X books per month, I prefer to block a specific amount of time on the calendar that I dedicate to reading per day. I'll generally spend 10 am to 1 pm just reading.

What systems can I use for organizing and storing information?

Consider all of the fleeting information that you deal with on a daily basis:
- Highlights from books, blogs, and so on
- Notes from YouTube interviews, podcasts, audiobooks, and so on
- Notes from conversations with people over coffee and meetings generally
- Notes you've written in journals and scraps of paper

Further to this, you also have your own thoughts that are not fully formed but might want to revisit later as well as reflections, general observations and ideas.

Finding a good system for managing this information flow such that they can be useful for us in the future can be powerful. Our human brain is amazing for a lot of things but remembering and recollecting specific bits of information is generally not among them. That's certainly that case for me so I like to use various note-taking systems. David Allen once said that *your mind is for having ideas, not holding them.*

Zettelkasten

Every note is just an element in the network of references and back references in the system, from which it gains its quality. — Niklas Luhmann

I personally like using a modified version of the "zettelkasten" system which was developed by a 20th century German sociologist named Niklas Lumann.

Lumann was highly prolific during his career. He authored almost 58 books and more than 400 articles during his lifetime on a wide variety of subjects including sociology, mathematics, biology and computer science, despite a relatively late start in life. His books have become classics that have made him a well-known sociologist.

A big part of his success across so many disciplines is due to a system he devised called *zettelkasten* (German), or the slip-box (a box filled with slips of paper). He considered his output to be relatively effortless thanks to his unique note-taking system.

The slip-box is at its core a system for storing and organizing knowledge, extending memory and generating new connections and ideas.

Lumann developed this system when he realized that any notes taken are only as valuable as its *context.* The idea is to be able to run into the right notes in a few months or a few years without actively searching for that particular note but instead for the context. I can have one tag "psychology" that has 5,000 notes which I'm obviously not going to scroll through each time I want to find something and that would render the tag "psychology" useless. Rather, if I'm looking at psychological biases, I might run into interesting notes I made years ago about decision making that I've long forgotten about. This is one way you can engineer serendipity. I would also use tags for projects that I'm working on or might be working on in the future so that I can stumble onto the notes again. The highly interconnectedness of notes within the slip-box is what makes it so powerful.

The slip-box is a simple system built on using paper index cards (zettel) and connecting the the cards thematically.

You can think of each zettel as a single note.

On one zettel is typically one idea which makes linking ideas together easier and can sometimes lead to unexpected connections. Each note should be autonomous in that it's self-contained and comprehensible on its own. Each note should also always be linked. Whenever a new note is added, always look for a way to link to existing notes. Briefly explain *why* you're linking the notes since you may forget the connection later on.

This linking has led notetaking software like Roam Research (the software that I use) and many others to include a feature called bi-directional linking to enable this connection. I've included a list of the most popular ones at the end of this book.

There are many great resources to learn about the zettelkasten system online including zettelkasten.de/posts/overview

FEEDBACK

Key Questions To Consider:

- How can I share my work?
- How can I get feedback and incorporate it into my learning process?

The best way to learn is not in a vacuum but with some form of feedback from the real world.

When a scientist has a hypothesis, they get feedback from their experiments. When an entrepreneur starts a business, they get feedback from their prospects. When a Knowledge Athlete acquires knowledge and produces insight, they get feedback from other knowledge workers.

One way to get feedback is to share what you've learned.

I follow this one person on Twitter that has been consistently sharing what he was learning about esoteric financial instruments and I noticed that he started to get some very valuable feedback from the financial Twitter community that he used to shape his understanding, and I can tell that it helped him grow tremendously.

While it's nice to have all of your accumulated notes and knowledge stored privately on your laptop, there's huge value in having other minds looking at whatever you're thinking about and working on.

If the idea of sharing your work in public feels daunting, you can start with those that will be more gentle like friends, colleagues and teachers. Eventually you can work your way towards a larger audience as you gain more comfort.

Other good avenues for getting feedback on your thoughts generally are mentors, mastermind groups, a personal/business coach, a therapist and so on. This is great just for making sure that your thinking and judgment is sound.

The Benefit Of Writing

There are many benefits to writing but one of them is that writing can be an important part of the *thinking process* and it takes place as much on paper as it does in your head.

By putting your work out in some kind of coherent form (an essay, a book review, a book etc.), you get to see any gaps in your own thinking. Things that made complete sense in your head may suddenly stop making sense once you're writing a long-form blog post. This presents a great opportunity for you to revise your thinking.

I wrote this book mainly to clarify for myself what it means to be a Knowledge Athlete as well as to share with you what I've learned.

An added bonus is that I've connected with like-minded people that are curious about the world and love learning as much as I do!

CONCLUSION

Outcompete in the knowledge economy by developing your edge.

Do the things that are **uniquely suited to you**.

- Am I being true to myself?

Stay with the **things that you love.**

- What do I naturally gravitate towards?
- What am I naturally curious about?
- How do I spend most of my free time?
- How would I spend my time in an ideal world?

Be committed and **stay consistent** for your repetitions to accumulate into a competitive edge.

- Where am I building my edge?
- Do I care about *how* I'm doing my work?
- Am I willing to iterate many times?
- Does the process *spark joy* for me?

You need to **stay focused**, **protect your mind** and **remove distracting thoughts.**

- Does the thought deserve to be here?
- Is it worthy of my precious brain cells?

- Why is this thought here?
- What are all of the things that can distract me?

There are no limits to what you can do. You can achieve almost **anything you want**, just not everything.

- What are my most empowering beliefs?
- What are beliefs that have held me back the most?
- Do I believe that anything is possible?
- Do I accept full responsibility for everything that happens in my life?

The order in which you do things matter. Time your activities optimally by understanding the rhythms of your body. **Know when to push hard, and when to rest well.** Both are important.

Pay attention to your environment. Optimize for flow.

Seemingly boring things like the right habits and routines, but done consistently well over time, will **compound into something magical**, the same way that knowledge compounds.

Don't be afraid to stay true to who you are.

Believe in your right to be here and to make your mark in this world.

Unleash your true potential by doing only what you can do best.

ADDITIONAL RESOURCES

Openlibrary.org

Free library of the internet.

Mostrecommendedbooks.com/people

Find out what Naval Ravikant, Bill Gates, and others you might follow are reading.

Whatshouldireadnext.com

Enjoyed a book and want to find another one like it? This site will help you find it.

Blas.com

Over 700 free book summaries.

NOTE-TAKING SOFTWARE

The software I personally use for note-taking is Roam Research.

I made a short introductory course to using Roam on SkillShare.com (you can get course on a 1-month free trial using https://www.skillshare.com/roamresearch).

Other good ones include:
- Obsidian
- Notion
- RemNote
- TiddlyWiki

ABOUT THE AUTHOR

Rui Zhi Dong is a recognized industry expert and the author of the best-selling book, *51 Questions That Changed My Life*. He is also an advisor to multiple technology companies.

Rui travels extensively, carrying his teachings throughout the world. He holds a Bachelor of Applied Finance from Macquarie University (2008).

He lives in Sydney, Australia.

www.ingramcontent.com/pod-product-compliance
Lightning Source LLC
Chambersburg PA
CBHW050319010526
44107CB00055B/2304